THIS COLORING BOOK BELONGS TO:

____

50 FASCINATING FACTS ABOUT THE OCEAN

The world's oceans have always been a place of wonder and mystery. Covering nearly three quarters of our planet, it's impossible to know all their secrets – but here're a few of the most interesting that we do know.

The surface

71% of earth's surface is covered by ocean

ROUND OUR OCEANS ARE COVERED BY SEA ICE

90% OF AN ICEBERG IS SUBMERGED BELOW THE WATER'S SURFACE

4.3x FASTER The speed sound travels underwater compared to air – this makes determining direction of sound near impossible for divers

The world's oceans aren't flat. Gravity affected by underwater mountain mass combined with winds cause sea level differences around the globe

200m (656ft) light scarcely penetrates the ocean at this depth

1,000m (3,280ft) most of the ocean is completely dark at this depth

10m BELOW THIS DEPTH DIVERS CANNOT SEE RED OR YELLOW – BLOOD APPEARS DARK GREEN IN COLOR

Point Nemo at 2,688km (1,670mi) from land, it's the most remote point in the ocean

3.8bn years ago Earth's temperature cooled allowing water to condense from gas into rain – filling the basins we know today

Blue oceans – water absorbs the red light of the color spectrum, leaving the blue for us to see

Nitrogen narcosis An effect causing divers to feel "drunk" occurring at a depth of 30m (100ft)

3bn years THE TIME LIFE ON EARTH WAS RESTRICTED TO THE OCEANS DURING EVOLUTION

1000 years time taken for water to complete a continuous journey around the world – known as the global ocean conveyor belt

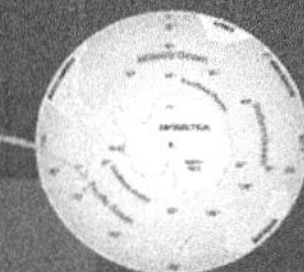

Warm surface flow

Cool subsurface flow

THE GREAT BARRIER REEF CAN BE SEEN FROM THE MOON

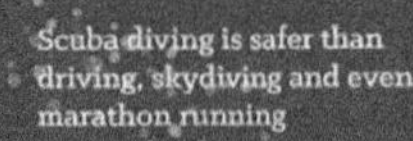

Scuba diving is safer than driving, skydiving and even marathon running

Diving deeper

97% of Earth's water is contained in its oceans

3,700m (12,100ft) the average depth of the ocean

10m (33ft) OF OCEAN DEPTH HAS THE SAME MASS AS THE ATMOSPHERE

1.35bn km³ The total volume of the world's oceans

2.5cm (1 inch) of the ocean depth has as much water as the atmosphere

2.5m (8ft) of ocean depth holds as much heat as the atmosphere

Dissolved gold can be found in the water of every ocean – but there's not too much of it

Half of the oxygen we breathe is produced by the ocean

50x MORE CARBON IS HELD IN THE OCEAN THAN IN THE ATMOSPHERE

Ocean living

28 major groups of animals live in the ocean, whereas only 11 live on land

The longest known mammal migration was achieved by a gray whale traveling 22,511km (14,000mi) over the course of 172 days

230,000 marine species are known – with over 2 million estimated to exist

14% of protein consumption comes from fish

97% of earth's habitat space is found in the water covering the globe

Some species in the Antarctic have natural antifreeze in their blood to prevent freezing. Hákarl – one of the world's most acquired tastes – is a product of fermenting shark to allow the antifreeze toxins to rot away

FLOUNDER FISH CAN USE THEIR CAMOUFLAGE TO HIDE ON A CHECKERBOARD

Coral is actually a colony of tiny animals with porous limestone skeletons – suitable for repairing human bones

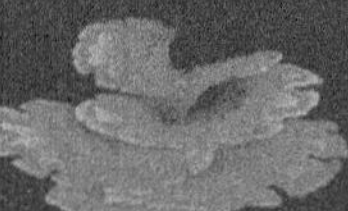

33m (108ft) the largest recorded blue whale (that's the height of an 11-story building)

6,000m the depth at which some species of deep-sea coral live (in waters as cold as 2°C)

1% OF THE OCEAN FLOOR IS COVERED BY CORAL REEF

25% of all marine species call these reefs home

Corals are greatly important to many marine species

They are slow growing – therefore it's crucial to never break or step on them

Deepest depths

5% of the ocean floor has been mapped in detail

BAHAMAS
where the **largest underwater cliffs on Earth** are found – with sheer drops of up to 4,000m (13,100ft)

65,000KM (40,300MI)
The length of the world's longest mountain chain – the Mid Oceanic Ridge which joins up around the globe like a seam on a ball

TWICE AROUND EARTH
Length of all mid-ocean ridges of the world if combined

Many species that live at the bottom of the ocean – abyssal creatures – can **glow in the dark** by triggering special chemical reactions

11 km (6.8mi)
below sea level – the Mariana Trench in the Pacific Ocean is the **deepest depth currently known**

10 km (6.8mi)
The world's tallest mountain found in the Pacific Ocean, known as Mauna Kea

Mount Everest
8.8 km (5.5mi)

8,143m (26,715ft)
the deepest living fish ever recorded – nicknamed the "ghost fish"

8 tonnes / in²
The pressure in the Mariana Trench (1000x the atmospheric pressure at sea level)

-1 to 4°C
temperature in the Mariana Trench

Records

214m (702ft)
THE DEEPEST FREEDIVING (NO LIMIT) ACHIEVED, COAST OF SPETSES, GREECE 2007

11,000m (36089ft)
The deepest descent into the sea by manned vessel achieved in the Mariana Trench, in 1960

332.35m (1,090ft 4.5in)
the deepest SCUBA dive achieved, Red Sea, Egypt 2014

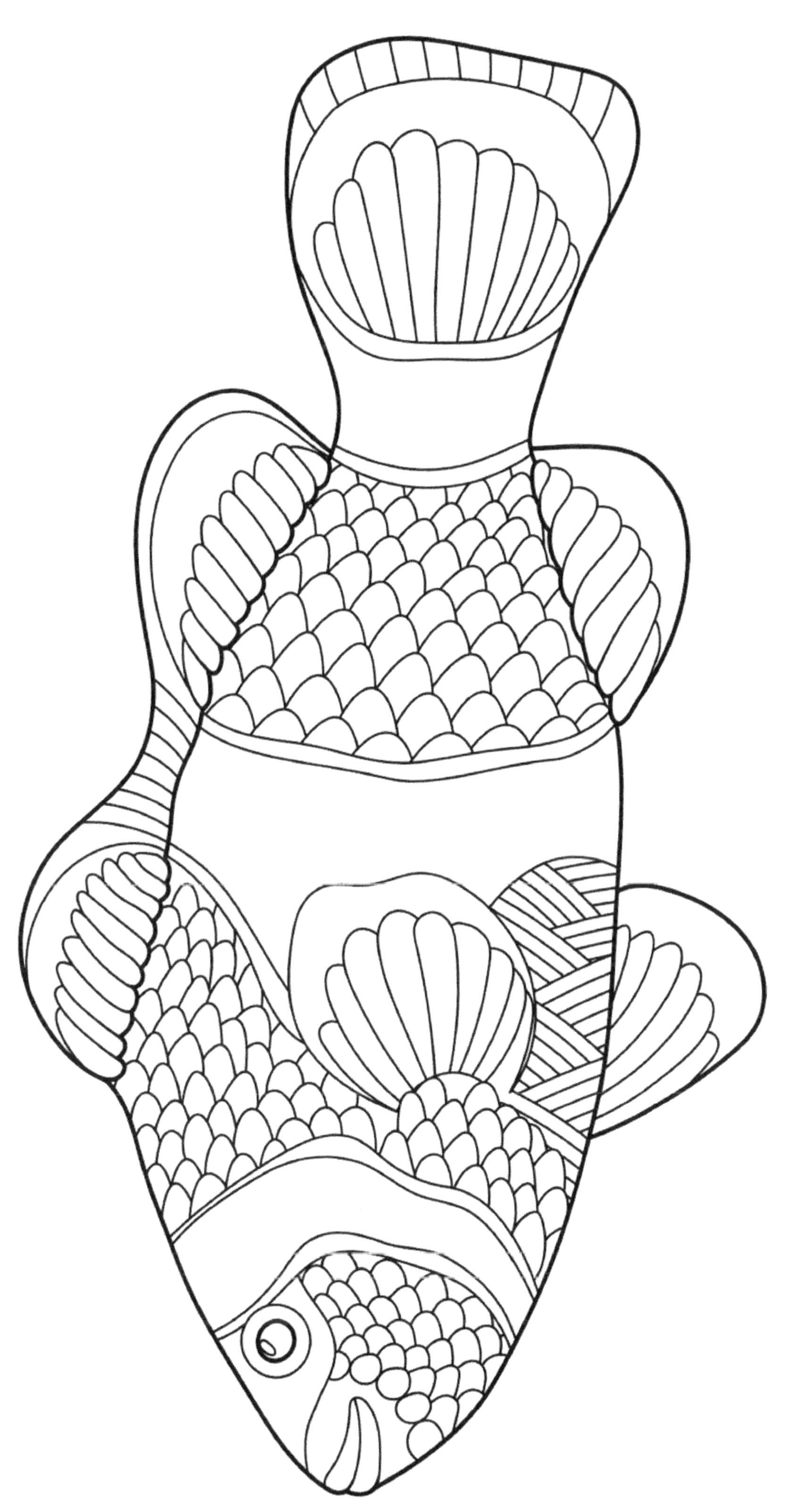

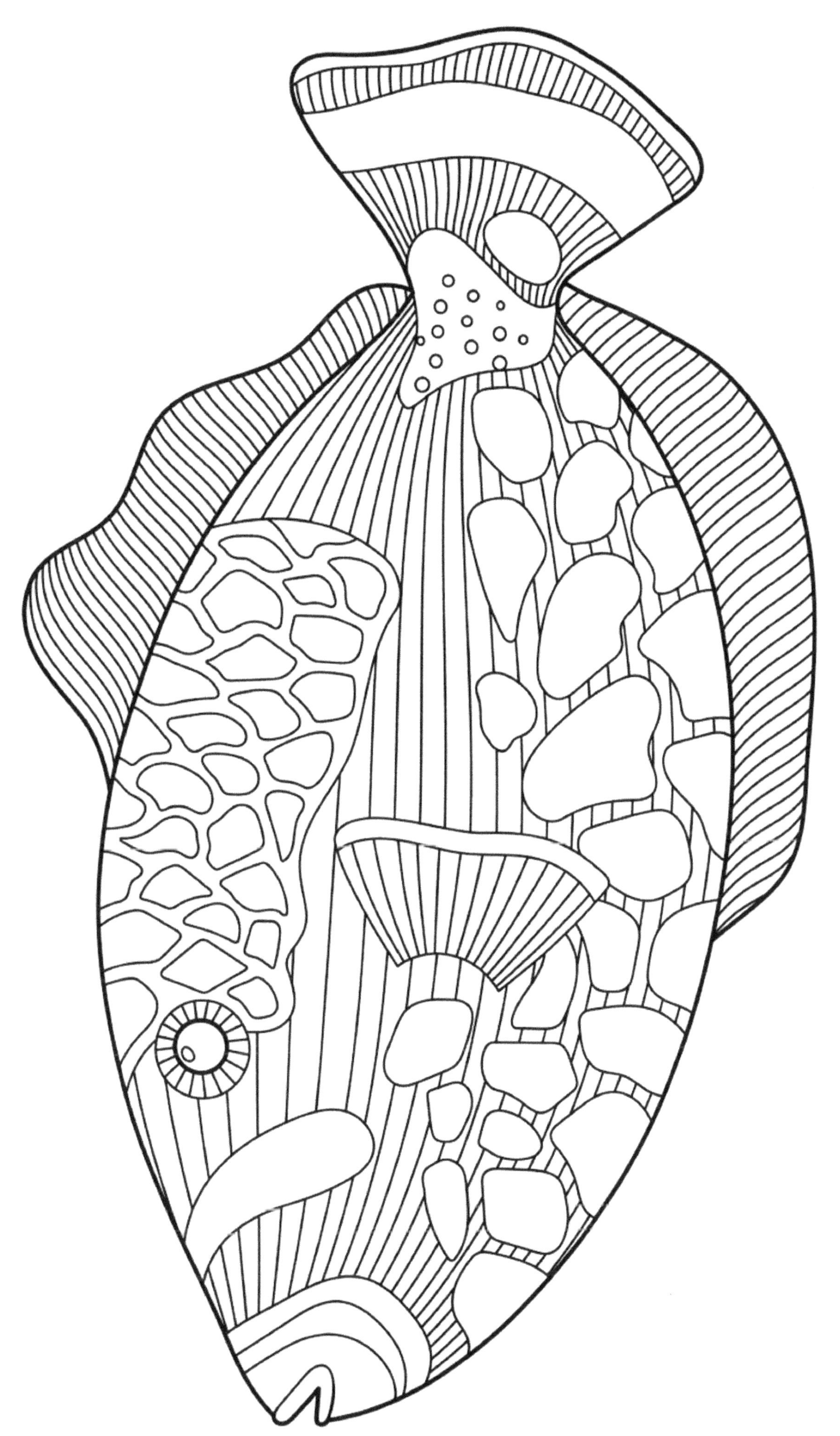

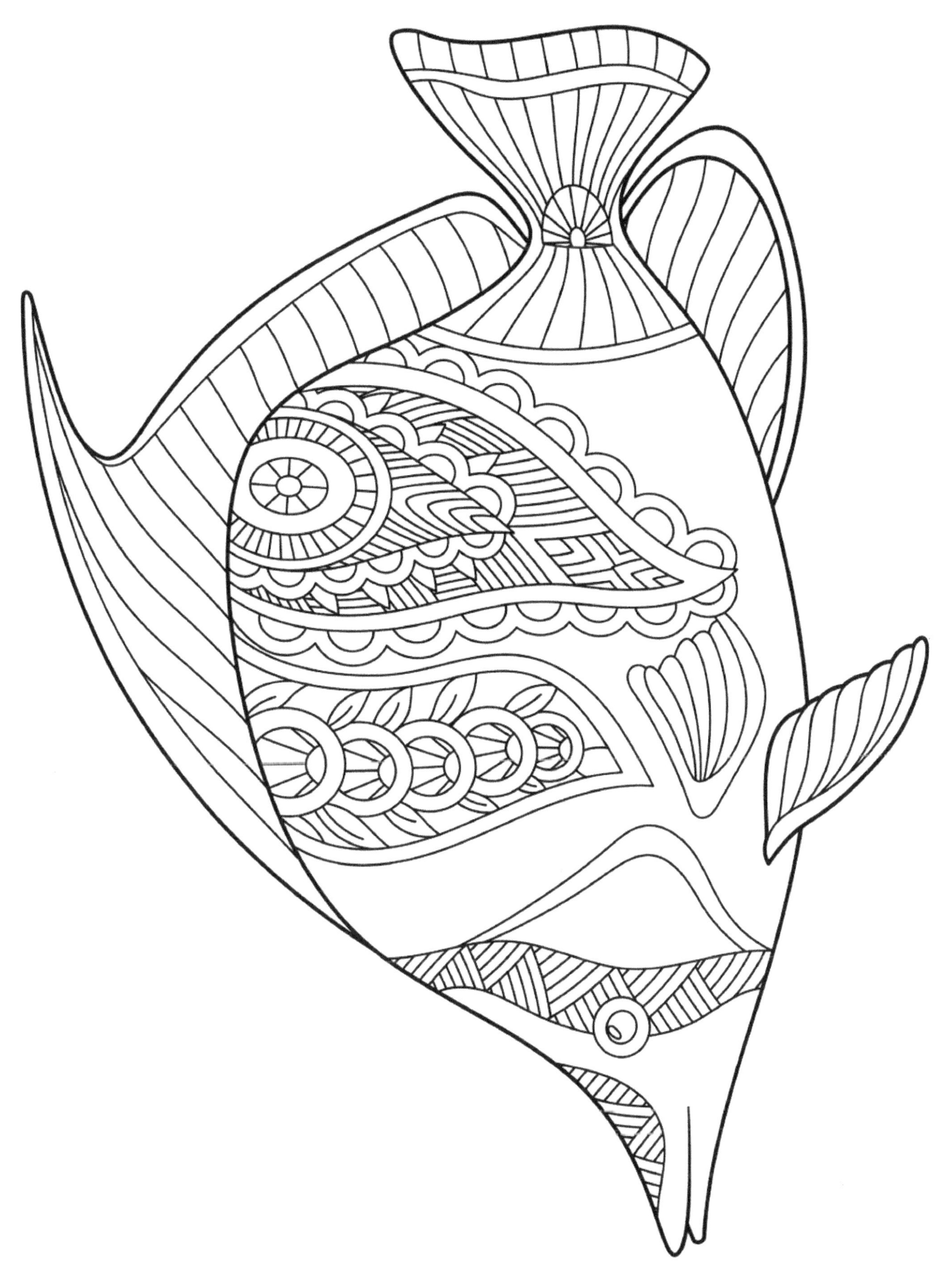

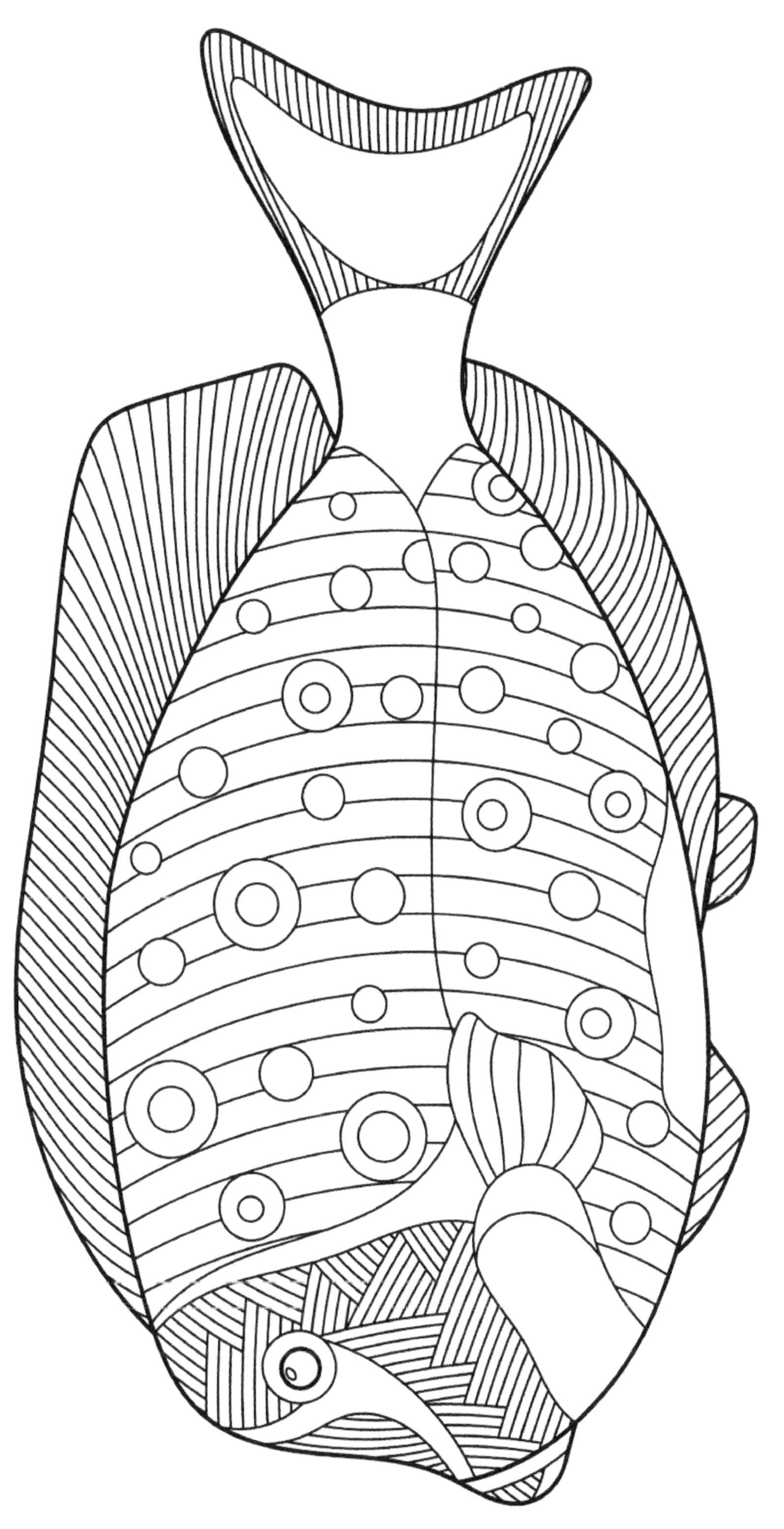

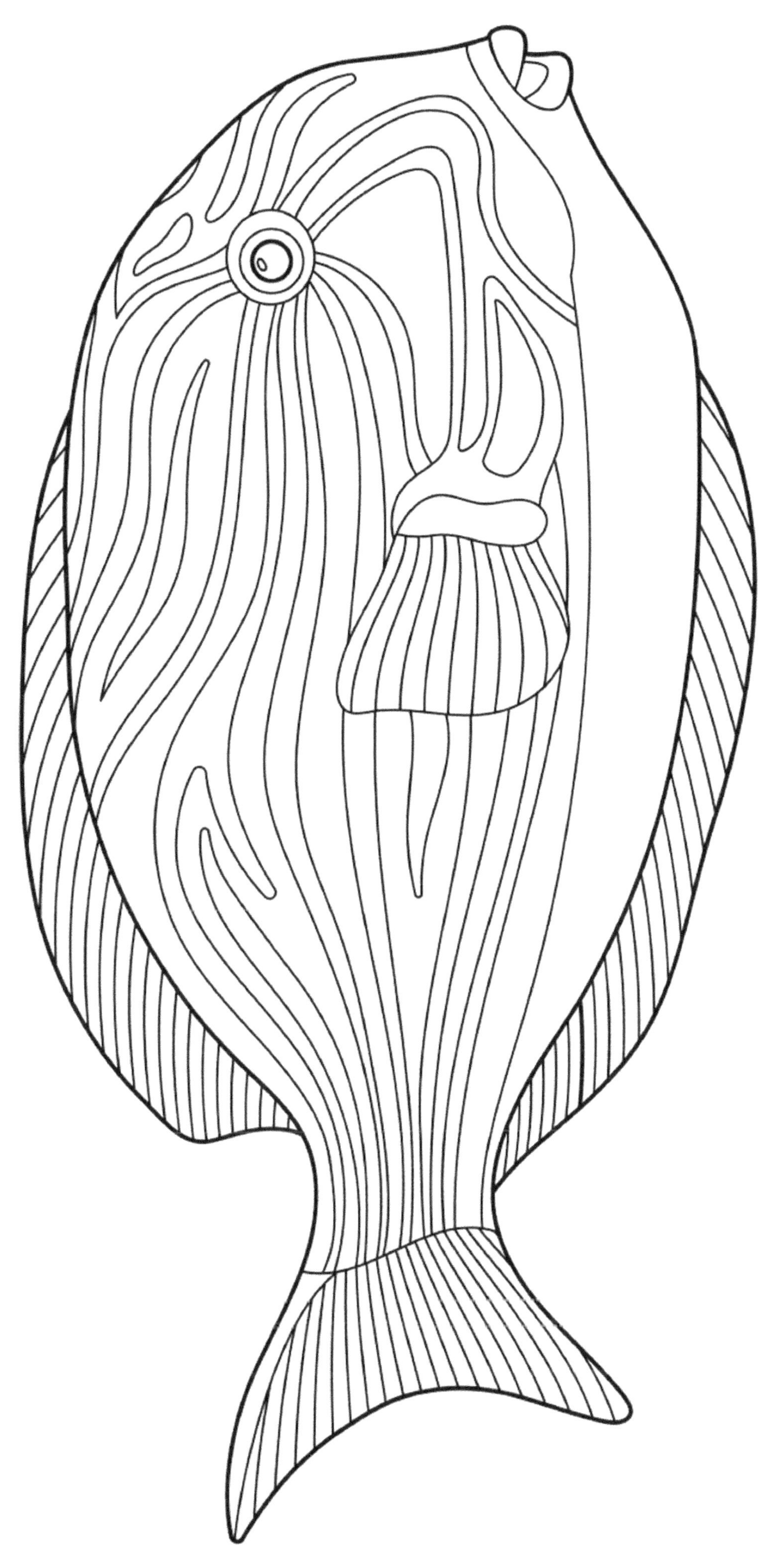

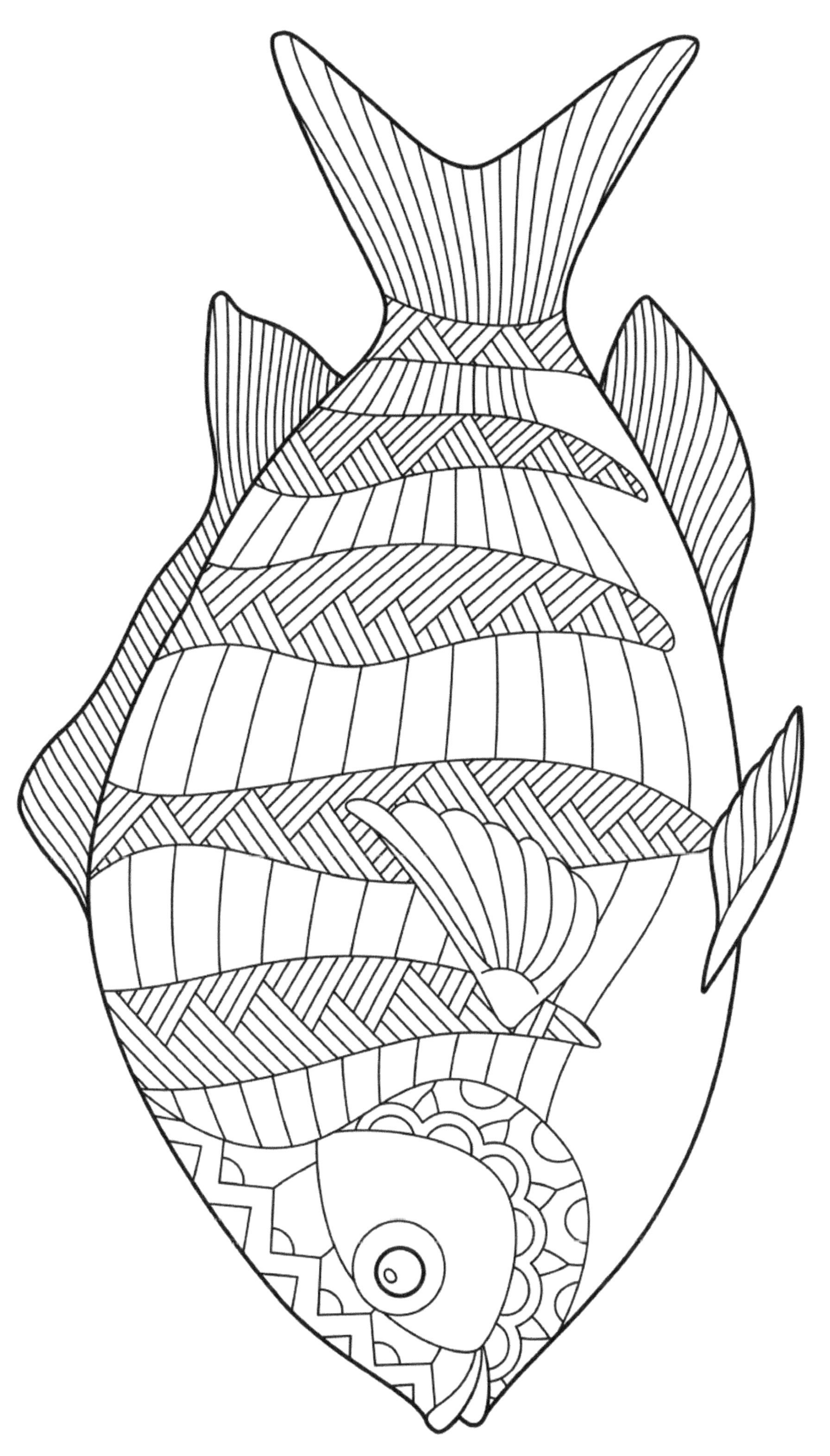

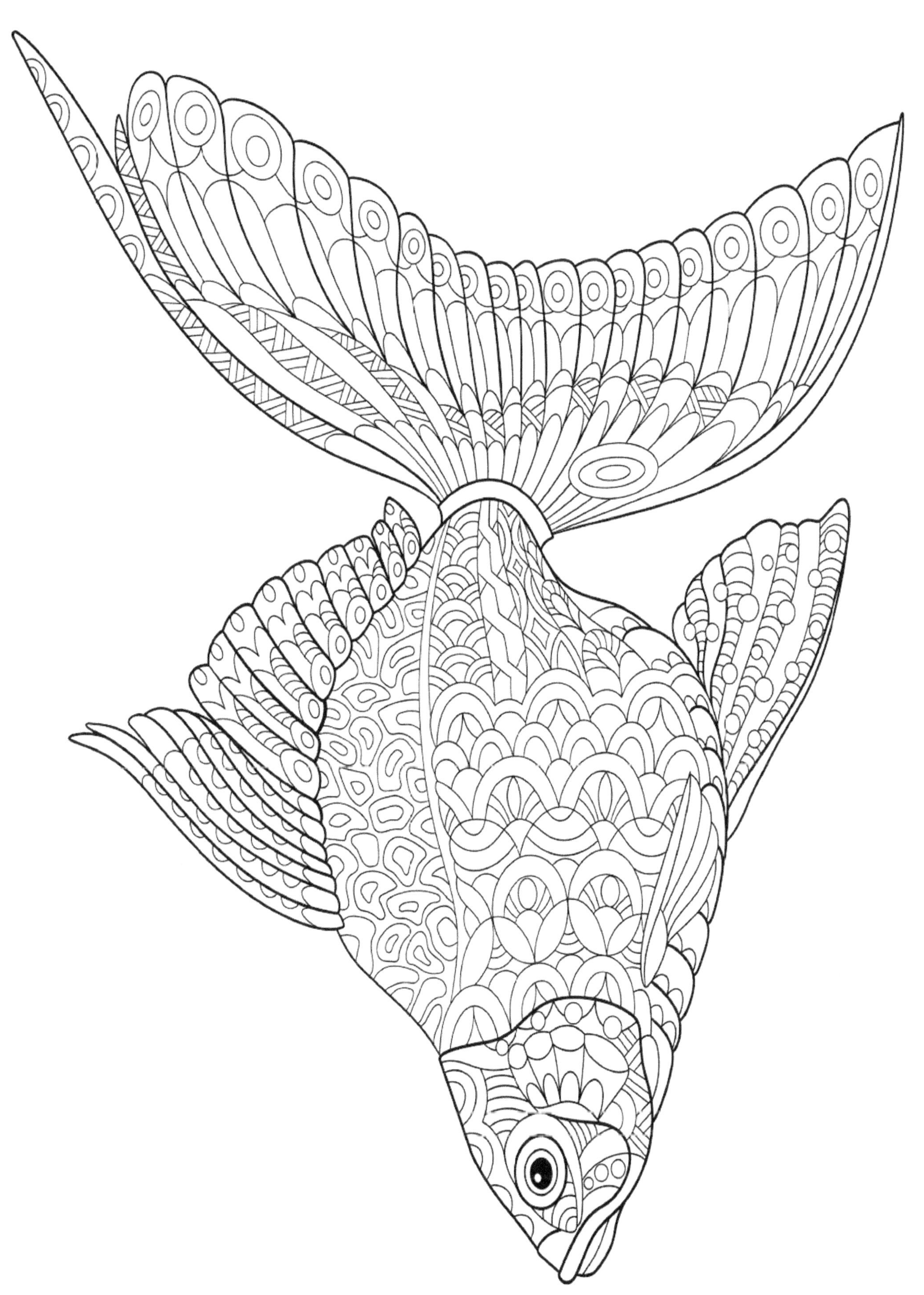

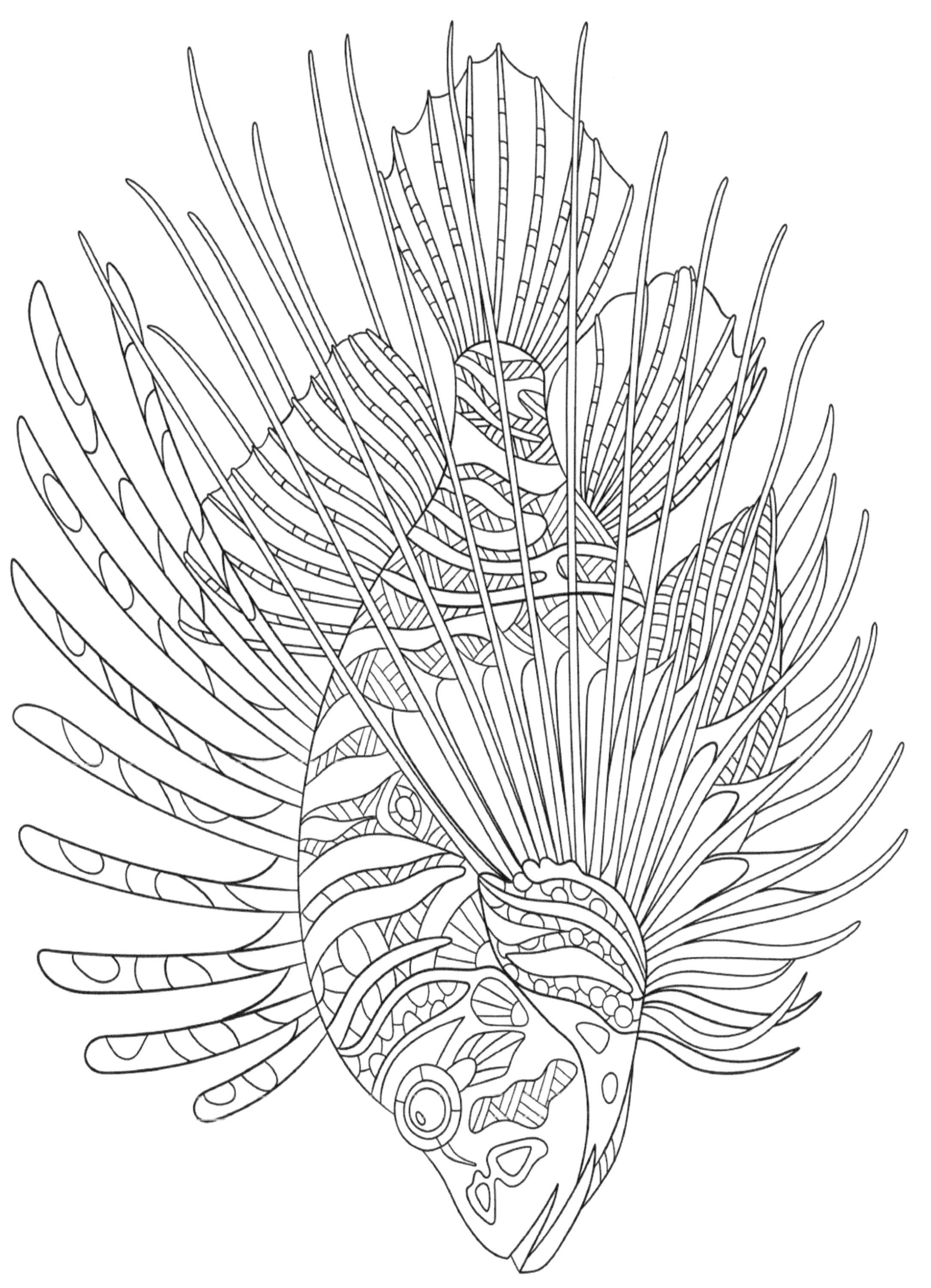

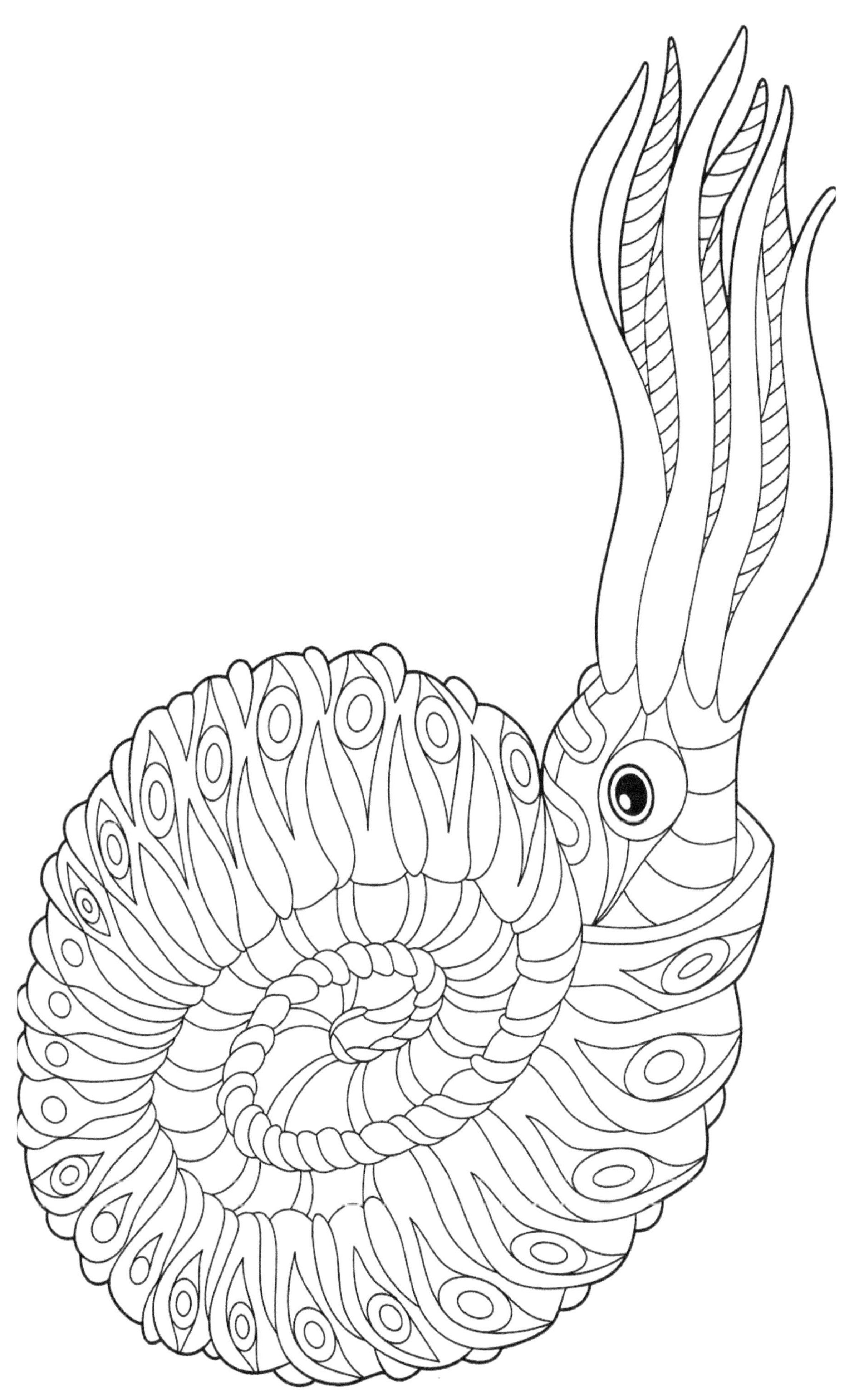

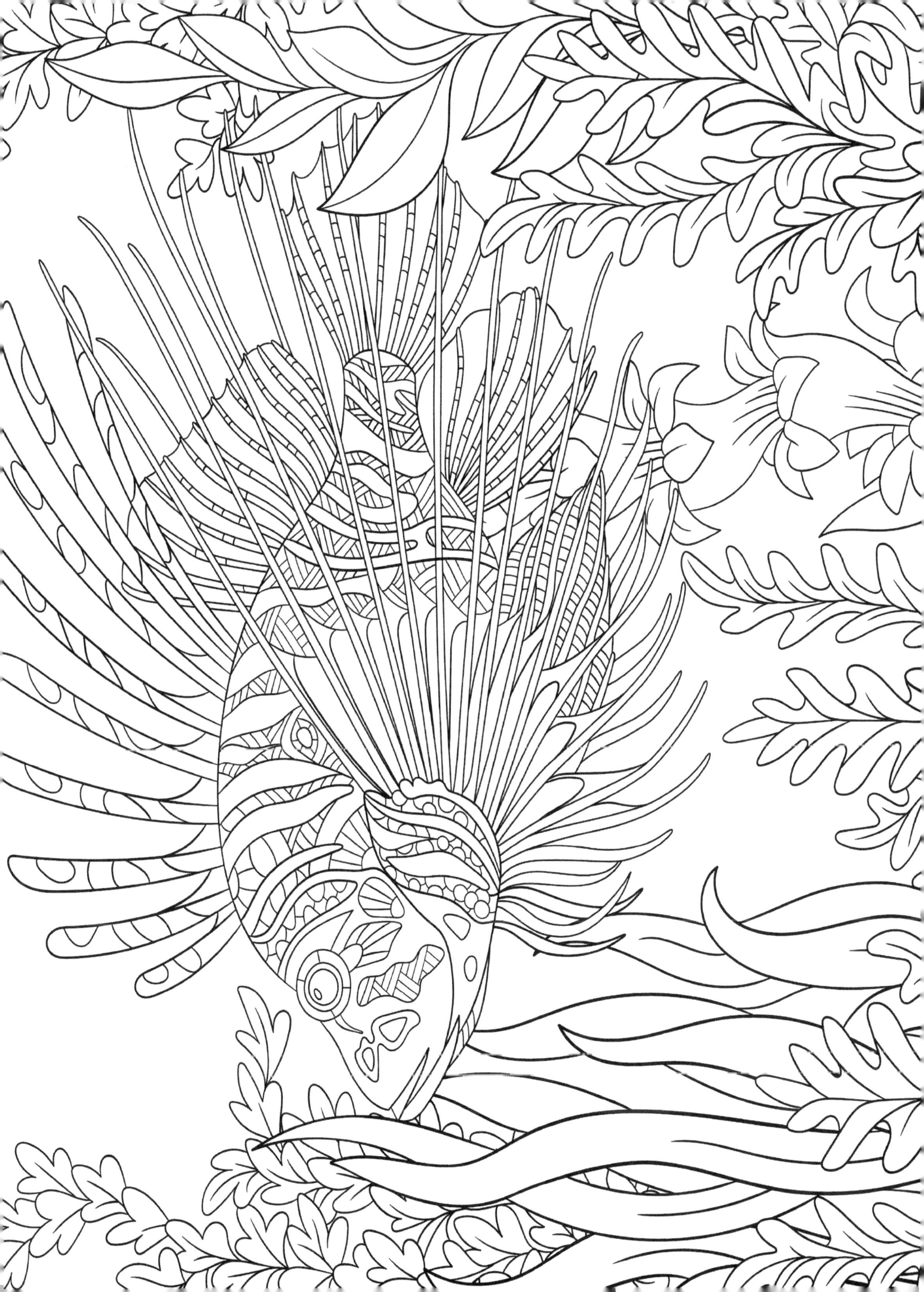

TUNE MY
HEART
TO SING THY
GRACE